T0390028

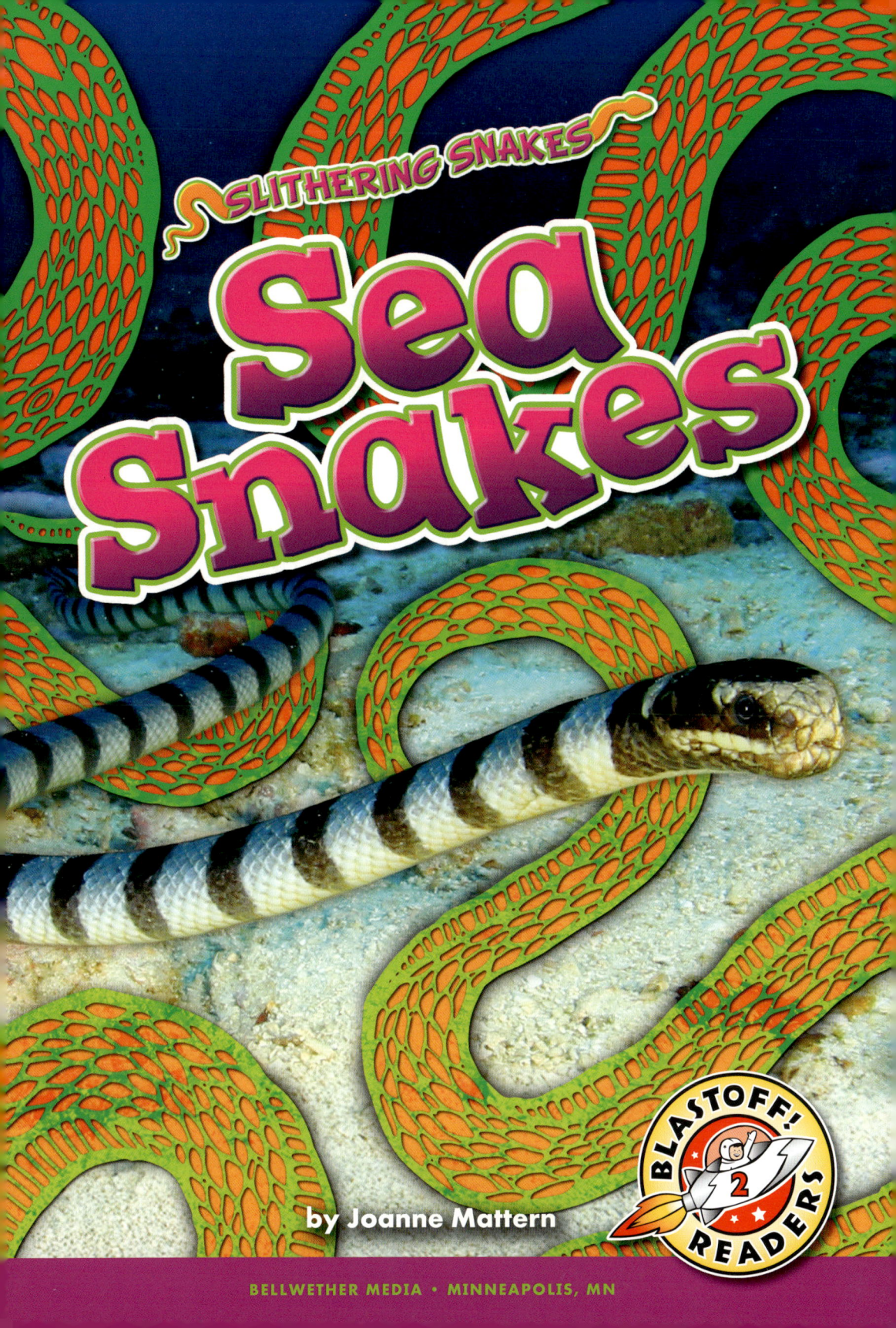

SLITHERING SNAKES

Sea Snakes

by Joanne Mattern

BLASTOFF! READERS

2

BELLWETHER MEDIA • MINNEAPOLIS, MN

Blastoff! Readers are carefully developed by literacy experts to build reading stamina and move students toward fluency by combining standards-based content with developmentally appropriate text.

Level 1 provides the most support through repetition of high-frequency words, light text, predictable sentence patterns, and strong visual support.

Level 2 offers early readers a bit more challenge through varied sentences, increased text load, and text-supportive special features.

Level 3 advances early-fluent readers toward fluency through increased text load, less reliance on photos, advancing concepts, longer sentences, and more complex special features.

★ **Blastoff! Universe**

Reading Level

Grade **K**

Grades **1–3**

Grade **4**

This edition first published in 2026 by Bellwether Media, Inc.

No part of this publication may be reproduced in whole or in part without written permission of the publisher. For information regarding permission, write to Bellwether Media, Inc., Attention: Permissions Department, 3500 American Blvd W, Suite 150, Bloomington, MN 55431.

Library of Congress Cataloging-in-Publication Data

LC record for Sea Snakes available at: https://lccn.loc.gov/2025001562

Editor: Kieran Downs   Designer: Brittany McIntosh

Printed in the United States of America, North Mankato, MN.

Table of Contents

Swimming Snakes

yellow-bellied sea snake

There are more than 60 **species** of sea snakes. Most are called true sea snakes. Some are called sea kraits.

Sea snakes live in warm oceans around the world.

Yellow-bellied Sea Snake Range

N
W E
S

range = ▢

Most sea snakes are around 4 feet (1.2 meters) long.

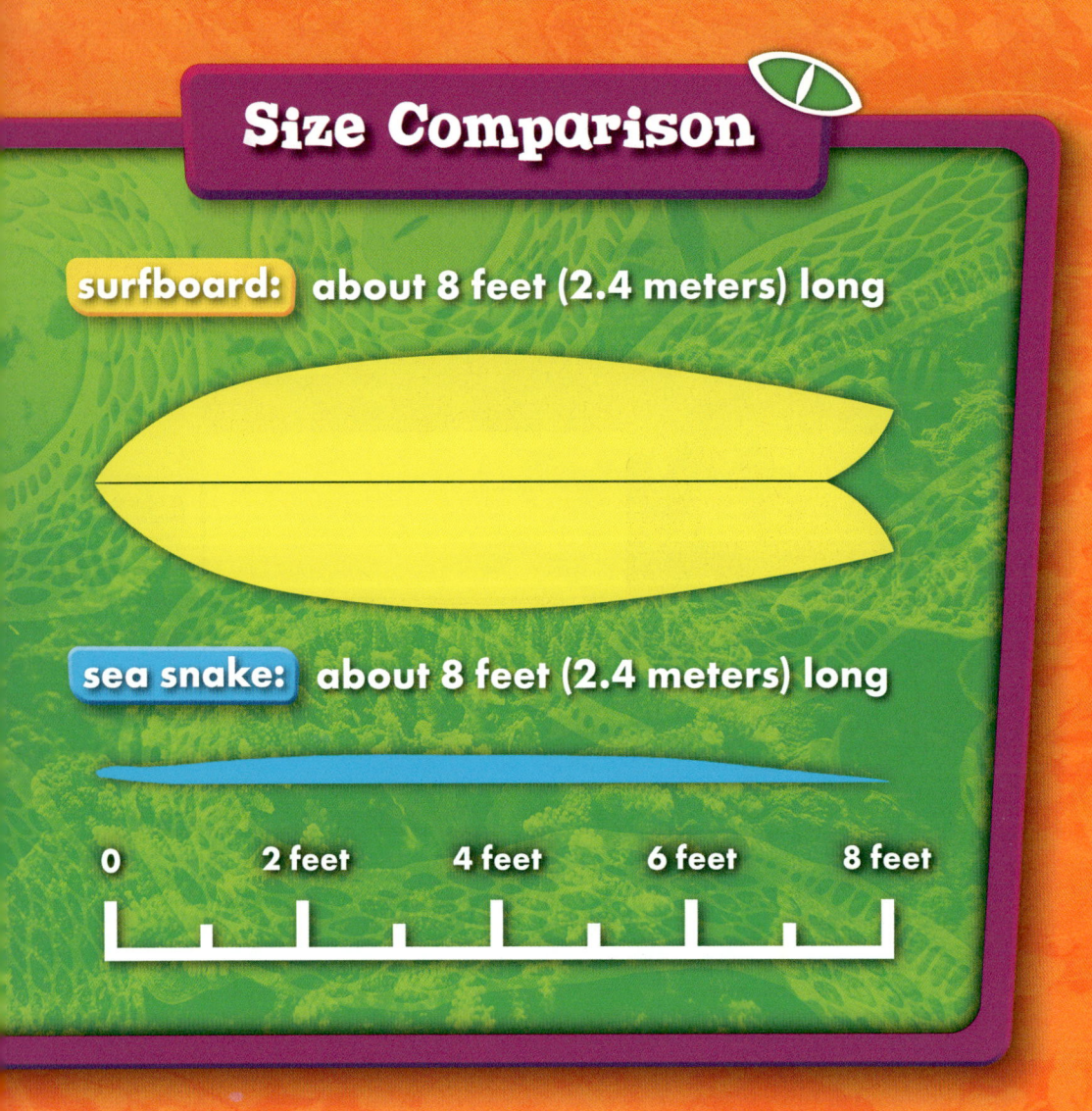

Size Comparison

surfboard: about 8 feet (2.4 meters) long

sea snake: about 8 feet (2.4 meters) long

0   2 feet   4 feet   6 feet   8 feet

yellow-lipped sea krait

But some can grow to over 8 feet (2.4 meters) long.

black-banded
sea krait

Most sea snakes have flat bodies. Their oar-shaped tails help them swim.

These snakes can be many different colors including red, yellow, and black.

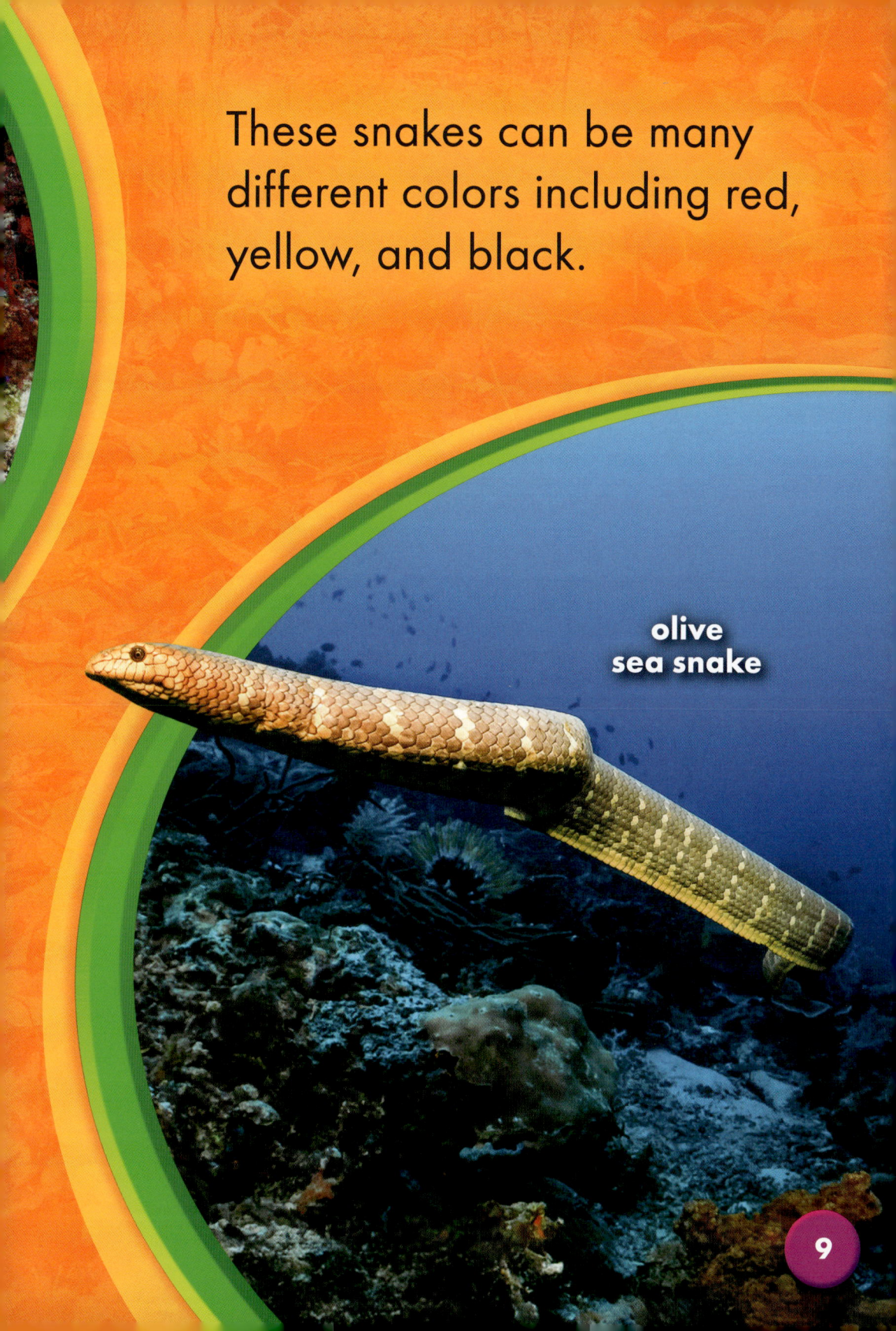

olive
sea snake

nostril

Sea snakes swim in salty water.
A special **gland** takes salt
out of their bodies.

Sea snakes breathe through their skin underwater. They breathe air through small **nostrils** when they surface.

Spot a Sea Snake!

small nostrils

oar-shaped tail

flat body

Life Underwater

Sea snakes live in **shallow** waters. They like to live alone.

Sea snakes can stay underwater for up to eight hours. They spend most of their time hunting.

Sea snakes hunt with their sharp **fangs**. They carry a powerful **venom**. The venom quickly finishes off **prey**.

Sea snakes eat fish and eels. Some eat fish eggs.

Sea Snake Food

damselfish

butterflyfish

moray eels

15

Sea snakes have many **predators**. Sharks often eat them. So do eagles and ospreys.

predator

16

camouflage

Sea snakes swim away from danger. Their colors help **camouflage** them.

Land and Sea Babies

Most true sea snakes give birth in the water. They give birth to live babies.

18

Sea kraits lay eggs on land.
The babies **hatch**.
Then they swim away.

Baby sea snakes can take care of themselves right away.

They swim and hunt in the water, just like their parents!

Yellow-bellied Sea Snake Stats

status in the wild: least concern

life span: up to 10 years

Glossary

camouflage—to hide by using colors to blend in with the surroundings

fangs—long, sharp teeth

gland—a body part that makes a substance that the body uses

hatch—to break out of an egg

nostrils—the two openings of the nose

predators—animals that hunt other animals for food

prey—animals that are hunted by other animals for food

shallow—not deep

species—kinds of animals

venom—a poison produced by an animal

To Learn More

AT THE LIBRARY

Davies, Monika. *Deadly Sea Snakes*. New York, N.Y.:
Gareth Stevens Publishing, 2023.

Mattern, Joanne. *Rat Snakes*. Minneapolis, Minn.:
Bellwether Media, 2025.

Shaffer, Lindsay. *Sea Snakes*. Minneapolis, Minn.:
Bellwether Media, 2020.

ON THE WEB

FACTSURFER

Factsurfer.com gives you
a safe, fun way to find
more information.

1. Go to www.factsurfer.com.

2. Enter "sea snakes" into the search box
   and click 🔍.

3. Select your book cover to see a list
   of related content.

Index

The images in this book are reproduced through the courtesy of: Rich Carey, front cover, pp. 3, 11; NickEvansKZN, p. 4; frantisekhojdysz, pp. 7, 23; ReinhardDirscherl/ Alamy, p. 8; Blue Planet Archive/ Alamy, pp. 9, 13; Roland Seitre/ Nature Picture Library, p. 10; Ethan Daniels, p. 12; marinuse - Underwater/ Alamy, p. 14; Karoli Pow, pp. 14-15; Alf Jacob Nilsen/ Alamy, p. 15 (damselfish); Pavaphon Supanantananont, p. 15 (butterflyfish); Wet Lizard Photography, p. 15 (moray eels); michaelgeyer_photography, p.16; imageBROKER/ Michael Weberberger/ Getty, p. 17; Juergen Freund/ Nature Picture Library, p. 18; Jean-Paul Ferrero, p. 19; Travel Telly, p. 20; adrian hepworth/ Alamy, pp. 20-21.